Walks in Devon

CHRISTINA GREEN

SPURBOOKS LIMITED

Published by
SPURBOOKS LIMITED
6 Parade Court
Bourne End
Buckinghamshire

At the time of publication all footpaths used in these walks were designated as official footpaths, but it must be borne in mind that diversion orders may be made from time to time.

Sketch maps are not necessarily to scale.

ISBN 0 904978 12 5

Printed by Maund & Irvine Ltd., Tring, Herts.

Contents

WALK 1

IDEFORD.

3 loop walks of 2½ miles, 2½ miles and 3¼ miles.

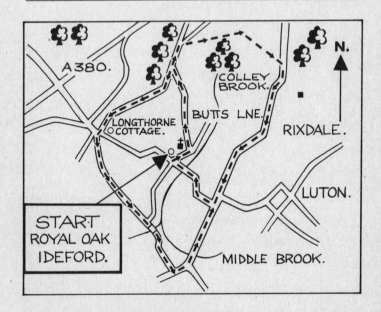

How to get there: By bus from Exeter or Newton Abbot.

Refreshments: In the Royal Oak, Ideford.

Half a mile off the humming A380 road to Exeter from Newton Abbot is Ideford, a gem of a rural village. Not obviously spectacular, its picturesque parts are tucked away and must be sought out to be appreciated. It is a splendid centre-piece of medieval paths and pack-horse routes, and there is some very pleasant walking to be had through quiet lanes and old bridleways, which may be muddy in bad weather.

The Royal Oak is a true village pub with excellent bar snacks. It has a large car park. On Wednesdays and Saturdays a bus from Newton Abbot will take you to Ideford, and on weekdays the Express Bus from Exeter will put you down half a mile from the village. Cars may be parked on the verge of the road outside the Royal Oak; until recently a magnificent turkey oak dominated the scene, but now the village awaits the transplantation of a new tree to replace the old one, so sadly found to be diseased.

The first loop walk of 2½ miles takes us from the Royal Oak along the road to the left, passing the church dated between 1300 and 1500. Notice the carved stone fixed to the outside wall of the chancel, which has been dated about 1100 and proves that an earlier Norman church stood on this site. The stone is a door lintel, depicting a dragon and a pelican, a bird often so connected with the early Christian faith. This church had many alterations made to it in the 16th century and again in more recent times. The additions harmonize well with the original stone, as the Red Quarry, near Ideford Arch, (just off the main road) provided all the materials.

After passing the church, the road twists left up a hill, but the name of the lane continuing straight on—Butts Lane— has links with the past, for here, on the water meadows to our right, the archery butts were set up for weekly practice.

The hill we take is a steep one, but has the saving grace of magnificent views through various gateways. These fertile lands slope down from the last ridge of Haldon Hills above us. On the left the patchwork of coloured fields runs gently down, leading the eye towards distant Newton Abbot, with the hump of Denbury Camp beyond, and finally to the high curving line of Dartmoor etched against the sky.

At the top of this hill the ancient trackway runs down to the left, full of memories of the Saxon Ida, who came this way, and founded the village when he crossed the ford down in the valley. Turn left and down this old path for an alternative loop back to the village, passing the fourteenth century cottage, Longthorne, at the junction of the road with the track, and following the track slightly to the left on the opposite side of the road. This descends, via rather uneven ground, to a lower road where a barn stands in a wide saucer of rich farm land, and Larcombe Bridge spans the little Colley Brook as it meanders through the fields.

5

The road to the left returns directly to the village if desired, but a further loop may be followed by continuing along the track, having passed Larcombe Bridge, and keeping to the left at the next fork. This is the old packhorse route to Bishopsteignton and Teignmouth. It joins a hill running down left to the stone bridge, and this road, signed to Ideford, brings us to another junction, where we turn left again and re-enter Ideford.

The alternative loop, however, from the junction of the hill past the Church and the old Saxon track, is to turn right, uphill beneath beech trees, and then turn right again into a track running beside fenced outbuildings and sheds. Once past the compounds this path bears left and joins a flint path running generally eastwards through Ideford Common, with magnificent oak trees below. In these woods, bubbling through a deep gulley, the Colley Brook rises, falling through fields until it reaches the village and Larcombe Bridge, crossed on our alternative loop, below.

The flint path continues across the Common between heather and occasional spruce trees, with one large tree much in evidence on our left. This, so legend says, was once used as a gallows and has given the Common its fancy name of One Tree Common. If this walk is timed for late afternoon, when the setting sun slips down behind Dartmoor, the colours are unforgettable.

Where the track meets the metalled road turn right and descend the hill, with glimpses of Haldon's high ground to the left. This loop walk is completed by turning right at the signpost at the bottom of the hill and returning the Ideford, passing farms and old cottages. Just inside the village the forge lies untidily by the roadside; here the first grass-cutting machine was made many years ago.

Once more at the Royal Oak, spare time to look at the cottages with old-world and historical names. Ideford has a lot to offer.

WALK 2

CHUDLEIGH.
A 3 mile loop walk, with an alternative 4 mile loop walk.

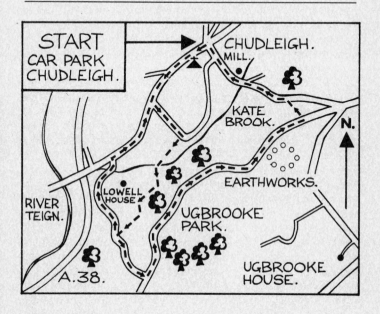

How to get there: By bus from Newton Abbot, or by car.

Refreshments: In Fore Street, Chudleigh.

    Chudleigh can be reached by the no. 1 bus from Newton Abbot, or by car via the A38(T) from Exeter. It is a small village where the wheel has turned full circle; the railroad has been and gone, and Chudleigh today, its traffic banished to the nearby A38, is quiet and peaceful, once more the "secret place" of its Saxon origins. Explore the narrow lanes of its countryside, the relics of past history hidden within the village, and see for yourself what delights Chudleigh has to offer.

7

There is a large free car park in the centre, with The Old Coaching House and the Bishop Lacey, as well as several tea rooms, to afford refreshment. From the car park Fore Street take us through a variety of shops and houses to St. Martin's Church, built originally in 1259 and consequently—and frequently—restored. The fire that swept the village in 1807 and destroyed 166 houses spared the church, and the Bishop Lacey across the road, once connected to the church by a passage. Next door to the church is the old Grammar School, built in 1668; note the stone in the wall.

Further along the road we turn left at the Police Station and pass Palace Farm, built on the site of Bishop Bartholemew's Palace, which dates back to 1080. Through the orchard gate a few fragments of masonry can be seen; there are tales of underground passages and dungeons, and in fairly recent excavations skeletons were found near the Quarry at the end of this road.

Our way takes the footpath off to the right, just before the Quarry entrance, and on up to Chudleigh Rock, which, together with wool, cider and chudleighs (buns), has made the village famous. This is awkward walking, along muddy, twisting, sometimes overgrown paths, and no specific directions can be given; on the assumption that all paths lead to heaven, take the track that climbs, and with any luck you should arrive at the top—avoiding the precipitous side of the Rock which lies close to the path. Enjoy the wonderful view from this sunny spot before turning left into the trees and exploring the paths which lead down to Kate Brook. Here, among overgrown bushes and immense trees, the stream plays along, tumbling eventually into a spectacular waterfall.

Climbers and potholers devote much time to the Rock, and even though the rambler is not disposed to join in such activities, the Pixies' Hole must be seen. This deep cavern has two claims to fame; Coleridge wrote about it, and the pixies claim it as their own.

Leaving the woodland surrounding the Rock behind us, we come out into a lush meadow. Follow the track around the perimeter, running alongside the Brook, and cross the bridge. Now follow the wire fence which joins the fence of Lawell House. Continue along through a field dotted with huge oaks.

Looking back, Chudleigh Rock stands out handsomely against a backdrop of sky and foliage.

The nearby A38 hums and roars, but here all is serenity, the quiet fields and woods seemingly untouched by the centuries. We pass over two stiles, walking under an avenue of lime trees, until we emerge into a twisting lane. Here the loops divide up, the shorter one turning right, and then right again at the road junction, and returning to Chudleigh by a straight route.

The longer loop, however, turns left into the twisting lane and winds up the hill. The tiny hamlet of Gappah, where once the gentry of Newton Abbot lived, lies to the right, but our way is to the left, following the ivy-clad wall running along beside us.

The road meanders between a splendid variety of trees, often merging into a green tunnel. On the right, amid its 600 acres, surrounded by lakes and hills, stands Ugbrooke House, the home of the Clifford family. Originally called Ucga's Brook, it was built by the first Thomas Clifford in the 17th century. The poet Dryden was a constant visitor to this estate and is said to have composed several of his poems here. Behind the wall we can see land climbing steeply to the Castle Dyke, a circular camp attributed to the Danes, with outworks of a later date. On the left the woods enclose the Quarry; when the trees end there is a bird's eye view of the village and the surrounding countryside.

An unmarked footpath, through a green gate, runs down across a field to Clifford Street, joining the road just above the cemetery. On the opposite side of Kate Brook, just above the bridge, stands Town Mills. Spare time here to browse and recall the past. Restored only recently, this old building retains the atmosphere and machinery of its historical life. An excellent booklet is on sale in the Mill, which is open to the public from 10 a.m. on most days, and on the floors above the mill-wheel is set out a Pandora's box of the best of hand-produced crafts in the British Isles, while the history of the village is depicted in a clever cut-out form, together with photographs and documents which help to bring the past alive again.

Clifford Street winds narrowly back to the centre of the village; the car park is opposite the junction of these roads.

WALK 3

THE RIVER LEMON
AT
NEWTON ABBOT

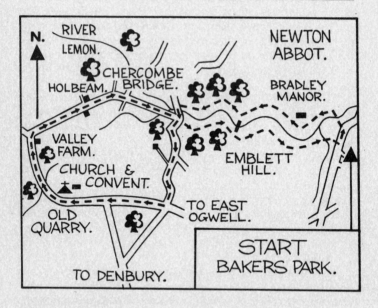

How to get there: By 15 or 88 bus from Newton Abbot.

Refreshments: In town centre.

A thriving market town, and an excellent centre for reaching many of these walks by bus or train, Newton Abbot has some delectable National Trust countryside fringing its busy hub of roads and shops. This loop walk explores quiet woodland and typical meandering Devon lanes; the walk can be a mere amble along the River Lemon, or a longer walk arising out of the first 3 miles.

A stone's throw away from the noisy A381, on the road to Totnes out of Newton Abbot, is Bradley Manor, one of the oldest fortified Tudor houses in Devon. On the western edge of the town, it is open to the public between 2-5 p.m. every Wednesday from 1st April until the end of September. The no. 15 and 88 buses from Newton Abbot pass its gates.

Cars may be parked at any of the paying car parks in the town, and our walk commences in Baker's Park, where a path at the far side leads through enormous old trees to the banks of the River Lemon. Amid these loops and bends peace may be had for the asking, which is a pleasant thought when hot and sticky from shopping in Newton Abbot.

Towards the close of the last century, a perfume called Bradley Woods Bouquet was much in demand, sold by a local chemist; even if the woods don't immediately call this fragrance to mind the scenery still impresses. The woodland paths offer easy, pleasant walking; the road dwindles to a footpath following the river and crossing a field. At Ogwell Mill there is a ford and a footbridge. On the opposite side of the river (to be perhaps visited on the return trip) is the depression known as "The Pit". Twenty feet deep with rocky sides, now overgrown, this was the secret meeting place of the first Noncomformists, over 2 centuries ago. Rather than be forced to worship in a manner contrary to their consciences, they held their own services at "God's Own Temple" in the woods; this they continued to do until finally a chapel was built in the town.

Following the river on through the woods eventually we come to Chercombe Bridge, sitting prettily between massive beech trees, the deserted lime kilns in the surrounding woods recalling the days of over a hundred years ago, when this industry was at its height, and the land busy with working men.

This is the turning point of the shorter loop, when a return journey may be made back to Newton Abbot (approx. 1½ miles) on the opposite side of the river, emerging via the road to Bradley Manor on the main A381, a short distance above the starting place, Baker's Park.

A further loop may be added on at Chercombe Bridge by walking another 4 miles along quiet country lanes, always turning right and thereby describing a complete circle. This passes through West Ogwell's ancient farmsteads, bridges the tiny beginnings of Blackford Brook, and returns once again to Chercombe Bridge.

Leaving Chercombe Bridge behind, therefore, head southwest and then turn right. Along this road lies the Convent of the community of The Companions of Jesus the Good Shepherd, once a manor house standing in its own incomparable deerpark. The grounds of the Convent are private, but the tiny church of West Ogwell may be visited. It is thought possible that this church, sited on a mound with an oak wood surrounding it, may have a history of early Druid worship. All records are lost, so the imagination may be left to wander. One fact remains however—the overgrown hollow in the field opposite the church is all that remains of the quarry where the pink Ogwell marble came from. Some original stone can still be seen in the church.

This is very beautiful country, with spreading fields balanced by huge trees. These old roads twist and bend, weaving their various ways, and charming the walker by their serenity and lovely surroundings.

After passing Valley Farm, turn right, passing Holbeam and then keeping straight on until once again Chercombe Bridge hoves into sight. Then the river provides its opposite bank for the walk back to Newton Abbot.

WALK 4

DARTINGTON HALL

A 3½ mile loop, with added on walk around the gardens of Dartington Hall.

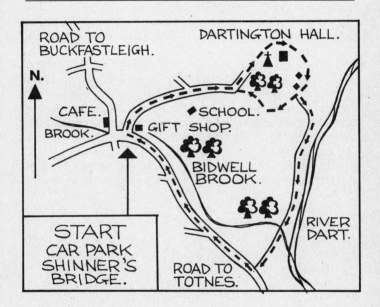

How to get there: By car.

Refreshments: At Dartington.

Sometimes as much pleasure can be derived from a leisurely stroll in semi-urban surroundings as an energetic hike over wild moorland; walking around the gardens and grounds of Dartington Hall can give this feeling of reward.

Shinner's Bridge in the village of Dartington, is some 2 miles beyond Totnes on the A384 road to Buckfast; now it is a restaurant, but once was the home of John Shynner in 1591, when the bridge was non-existent and there was merely a ford across the Brook. Here the pack ponies, loaded with wool and tin, passed on their journey from Ashburton to Totnes.

Our road winds up past Shinner's Bridge House, with the Dartington Hall Gift Shop on our right, and passes Dartington School before it bears right again at a small triangle. This quiet country road leads into the grounds of Dartington Hall, where there is a Gift Shop and a car park. The Gardens are open to visitors every day except Bank Holidays, and it is suggested that organised parties should apply to the Garden Superintendent for permission to visit. All seasons of the year have their own especial beauty here.

An archway leads into the courtyard, built in 1390 by John Holland, Duke of Exeter and half-brother of Richard II. From the courtyard a path winds towards the Gardens, passing the old kitchen wall and pausing at a lead urn. Take your pick of the numerous paths that curve away to the various enchantments of the Gardens. Wander at will and, even on a bedraggled winter day, you will find beauty at every turn. Summer foliage may be lovely, but equally so is the silhouette of bough and bare twig against a wild sky. Squirrels and birds go about their business in solitude; few tourists invade the Gardens, except in the height of the season, and usually only the passing student is seen.

Many spectacular views present themselves, every vantage point having, as it were, a different eye. Don't forget to search out the bronze donkey by Willi Soukop, and Henry Moore's reclining woman, which he described as " . . . a figure of quiet stillness and a sense of permanence as though it could stay there for ever . . . " Stare upwards at the vast 400 year old chestnuts lining the terrace that overlooks the jousting ground; appreciate the line of the 12 Apostles, the row of Irish Yews said to have been planted to screen a bear-baiting pit. Within the Gardens there are many lovely things, other than flowers, trees and shrubs; but the true climax of our wanderings must be found in the sight of the Hall itself, rising grey-stoned and handsome out of the subtle tones of the tiers of surrounding trees and shrubs.

Perhaps the most atmospheric part of Dartington Gardens is the 14th century church tower at the back of the courtyard, all that remains of the original church. This tower is now a chapel,

14

used by the College of Arts within the Hall. The enormous yew tree shading the old headstones is supposed to be a thousand years old; could there, therefore, have been an earlier Saxon church standing here before the 14th century? Dartington's earliest record dates back to 833. In 1878 the church was pulled down and rebuilt, some two miles away, from the old materials and in the same form. It stands now on the main Ashburton to Totnes road and is worth a visit.

The Gardens having been explored, we take the private road away from the Hall. This runs parallel with the River Dart, and crosses the Bidwell Brook, winding amid meadows and tree-lined fields, and brings us finally onto the main road, which, although seemingly countrified in its surroundings, bears much traffic and can be dangerous. Turning to the right from the private road, we return to Shinner's Bridge, approximately 1¼ miles along this Totnes to Buckfast road.

WALK 5

HENNOCK.

A loop walk of 5 miles, tough, demanding walking.

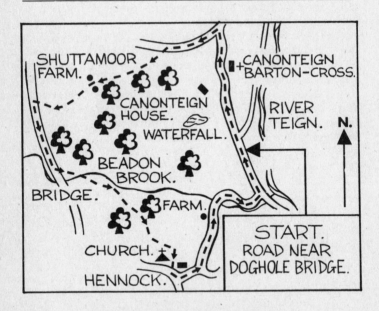

How to get there: By bus from Newton Abbot.

Refreshments: The Palk Arms, Hennock.

Hennock is a tiny, high-poised mining village in the Teign Valley, reached by winding lanes from Bovey Tracey, turning off the A38(T) from Exeter. The no. 44 bus from Newton Abbot calls there.

A walk amid this hilly, patchwork-coloured countryside is demanding, but has much to offer by way of reward. A good place to start—and to park cars on convenient verges of quiet country roads—is the old Tudor mansion of Canonteign Barton, a short distance along the Christow road from

16

Doghole Bridge on the west side of the River Teign. This "house of many gables", as an old book describes it, was left to crumble and decay for many years, but has happily just emerged from the hands of the restorers and is once more a private residence.

It was built in the first Elizabeth's reign and has experienced the occupation of two armies—the loyalist soldiers of Charles I, and, more recently, American Troops. The G.Is left peaceably, but the cavaliers defended their post against General Fairfax in 1645 and were defeated. Originally the seat of the first Viscount Exmouth, the house eventually became a farmhouse.

Tall, ivy-draped towers near the ruined gatehouse are believed to be the shafts of manganese mines; which came first, mine or house? And what is the history of the big granite cross standing in the grounds of Canonteign Barton?

We leave these mysteries unsolved and follow the lane passing North Lodge on the left, and then take a sharp turn left up the hill. Continue westwards, forking left through Bovey Forest and on down past Shuttamoor Farm. The map shows disused mine shafts to the west of the bridge at the bottom of the hill; indeed, the entire district is pitted with relics of mines and the enthusiast could spend much time exploring here.

The hill leads upwards to the reservoirs of Kennick and Tottiford, which feed Torquay. Here one is on top of the world, with a view to prove it. When the rhododendrons are in flower around the lakes the beauty is unsurpassable.

Turn left and follow the hill that now descends again, passing Tottiford farm standing in a lovely coombe with the Beadon Brook jaunting through it. Just before reaching Beadon Bridge turn into the forest track bearing left. Here the going becomes heavy with tangled undergrowth and fallen timber, not forgetting the usual quota of wet-weather mud. Cross Beadon Brook by the small wooden footbridge just before a further track commences to the left. Over the Brook start climbing again. Painted posts at regular intervals indicate the way; follow the track ascending towards Great Rock, almost at the top of the wood.

Further along the Brook there is a disused mine, with a wooden leat running parallel to the water through the

17

woodland. Although this leat is now mossed over and carries nothing more than dead leaves, it is a vivid reminder of the days when these woods, and the surrounding countryside, were a source of great mineral wealth.

Air shafts are shown on the 2½ inch map in the vicinity of Greatrock Copse and the adjoining fields. Follow the track as it climbs up and down, eventually the way resolving itself into a muddy road which—again!—winds up, finally joining the road into Hennock. There are some picturesque old cottages here and a handsome Church which is over 500 years old, with a tower 2 centuries older. Hennock suffered many deaths in the time of the Plague in 1546/7, as did other villages in this district.

The Palk Arms in the middle of the village will offer refreshment to the weary walker. The way home dives down the steep lane signposted Teign Village, forking left at Brandiron Cross, passing Franklands Farm, and taking in a good view of a disused mine chimney; finally crossing Hyner Bridge, and then completing the circle back to Doghole Bridge.

As a last attraction to a very lovely walk, there is the beautiful sight of the waterfall below Birch Cleave Wood, cascading down and forming an elegant backcloth to Viscount Exmouth's Georgian mansion, Canonteign House, on our left.

WALK 6

BOVEY TRACEY
2 loop walks of 2½ miles and 2¼ miles.

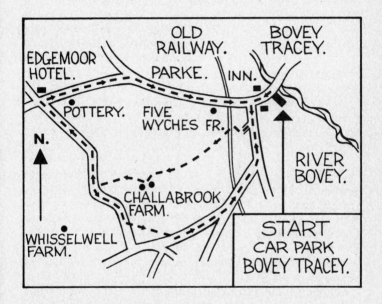

How to get there: By car.

Refreshments: In Bovey Tracey.

Bovey Tracey, one of the gateways to Dartmoor, is a small and pleasant village, full of history and lying in rich country at the foot of the Moor. It can be reached by taking the A38 road from Exeter to Plymouth and following the signposts.

The two loop walks are easy, on clearly defined footpaths and along country roads. Both start and end at the free car park in the centre of the village, on the bridge, between the Old Mill and the Old Dolphin.

Leaving the car park, turn left, perhaps, on a weekday,

pausing to visit the Weaving Shed of the Bovey Handloom Weavers on the opposite side of Station Road, and then passing the Dartmoor Hotel on the right. Turn left into Avenue Road at the side of the Central Garage. A brook burbles along beside the road, one of the feeder streams eventually running into the River Bovey.

At the T junction, where Fairfield Close joins Avenue Road, a footpath is signed to Chapple, via Challabrook Farm, and this is our way. Cross the old iron gates, with their warning of 40/- penalty for not shutting them, and go across the railway track, now hard-cored and bramble-hedged, and continue along the footpath through fenced farm land. Trees line the way, with tangled grasses falling over the accompanying brook.

A seat comes into view, and then a cross, with the plaque— "This old cross once marked the grave of a Royalist Officer who fell near here, 1645, when Cromwell's troops defeated the Royalists".

We cross the bridge, where the brook leaves us, and go through the gate into an open field, where the track is straight and clear. There is a view of Dartmoor here, the foothills striding away up to bare heights; the wind from the Moor often blows keenly here, a slap in the face after leaving the shelter of the footpath by the brook. Another iron gate, another field— and this time the view to the right shows us the impressive woods rising up to the heights of Hennock and its neighbouring countryside.

One more gate and we are in the approach to Challabrook Farm, with its attendant outbuildings. Farm cottages face us with a private sign indicating Right to Chapple, and asking "did you shut all gates?" and reminding that dogs must be kept under control. The footpath continues now to Chapple Road where we leave the farmlands and must decide which way to continue our walk.

If we turn left—a more urban end to our walk—a few yards along the road there is a seat on the bridged trackway of the old Granite Railway, over the brook. Laid in 1820, these clumsy stone trackways carried horse-drawn trucks for seven miles, bearing granite hewn from Hay Tor quarries down to the canal at Teigngrace. Here the barges were loaded and poled to Teignmouth, and the stones then taken by sea to London, where they were used to build part of London Bridge as well as many other public buildings.

Another 160 yards down the road to the left, we' take the Public Bridleway signposted. This is a continuation of the track seen earlier. At the end of the Bridleway turn left into Moor View, passing the Post Office, and continuing over the bridge; soon the Old Dolphin comes into view, with the car park beyond it.

The alternative loop, only slightly longer than the first, turns right at the junction of the foopath with Chapple Road. Sections of the Granite Railway appear all along the verge of this road, and the track is very evident before it disappears into Chapple Wood where one of the original milestones is said to be still in place.

Chapple Road takes us through a canopy of beautiful trees, uphill past a Bridlepath sign to Brimley via Whisselwell Farm, and continues on to a four crossway. The hill to the left goes to Hay Tor, this being the entrance to the Dartmoor National Park, but we turn right, passing the Edgemoor Hotel on our left as we go downhill. This old house, with its gracious grounds, was once Bovey Tracey Grammar School.

Some 60 yards on the right is Lowerdown Pottery, run by David Leach, and open to visitors Monday to Friday, from 9 to 1 and 2 to 6, and from 9 to 1 on Saturday. Continue down the hill, passing picturesque Five Wyches Farm and its old stone barn, both beautifully thatched with the thatcher's personal signature on each ridge.

This road, a seemingly quiet country road, is often busy with traffic en route to the Moor; walkers should be careful. At the junction where the old milestone stands, we turn right, continuing down into Bovey Tracey, where we pass the Dartmoor Gateway Restaurant. On the left is the remains of Bovey's old railway station, first run in 1866, now overgrown and alone with its memories and nesting birds.

The Dartmoor Hotel is on our right and at the junction, where the A382 to Exeter or to Newton Abbot is signed, we pass the Dolphin Hotel, which ran a coaching service in 1882, with four trips weekly over the surrounding moorland.

We cross the road, passing Brookside Tea Rooms and return to the Old Dolphin.

WALK 7

MORETONHAMPSTEAD.

Walk of 3½ miles with possible loop of extra ½ mile.

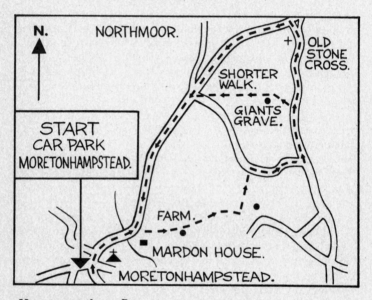

How to get there: By car.

Refreshments: In Moretonhampstead.

Moretonhampstead, on the A382 road from Bovey Tracey, or turning off the A30(T) at Whiddon Down, was once an important market town before roads and railways linked the moorland villages. Today its importance has faded, but an immense charm prevails. It snuggles in a bowl of fertile land on the fringe of eastern Dartmoor and is a splendid place for touring, and in particular for walking.

This walk is a quiet amble over (sometimes sticky) footpaths, twisting Devon lanes and a small chunk of open moorland. Where the Bovey Tracey road enters Moretonhampstead there is a large, free car park, and from here it is only a step to the centre of the village. A visit to the church is recommended, taking in en route the handsome almshouses, built in 1637 and still inhabited. Close by the churchyard once stood the famous Dancing Tree, where a platform was raised among immense branches to provide footing for a fiddler who played to the dancing villagers below. Cross Cottage now provides a memory of those festive occasions.

We take the road signed Mardon and Clifford and named "Lime Street to Kinsman's Dale" which surely gives an idea of the charm we are about to experience. Down the hill over the brook, passing a footpath signed to the left, and on an uphill bend we turn right, down a farm track signed Halscombe Farm. On the right, below the brow of the hill, set amid gracious gardens with rich trees and shrubs, stands Mardon House.

Follow the track and at Halscombe Farm take the **middle** path to left of an outbuilding standing below a farm cottage. The footpath, at this time of researching, was very overgrown and wet and sunken to a degree that, combined with trees meeting overhead, made the path seem like a dim, green tunnel. We go on, ever uphill. In places it is muddy with waist-high nettles, but always clearly defined. A pair of iron gates provides mouth-watering peeps of the countryside as we emerge from the tunnel. On and up . . . through a narrow stone gateway where once, perhaps, swung a kissing gate. Here we join another path ascending from the right. On through the trees, and a wooden gate then brings us to the road. Turn right. (Left is an entrance to private property).

At the gateway to Heathercrest, right, a superb view can be enjoyed. A few yards further along turn left through a stone gateway and follow the wire-fenced footpath beside a hedge. Here again the grass is long and wet, but the path itself is clear. At a tumbledown stone stile we join Mardon Down. Look at the view—a semicircle of Dartmoor is laid out for inspection, with Moretonhampstead a grey cluster beneath us. This is wonderful country, with birds and insects abounding, and only occasional farming noises to break the serene solitude. A cart track leads us to the road, where we turn right and then left at junction. Half way down this road a track over

23

the moorland to the left is an alternative loop which will cut half a mile off the complete walk. This track leads to the site of The Giant's Grave cairn—a forbidding name, but only a few stones remain. The view from this point shows Dartmoor to the south and west, and the distant smudge of Exmoor to the north, far beyond the steep sides of the Teign gorge. This track continues down over the moorland and meets up with the alternative loop, which ignores the track via the Giant's Grave and goes on until tracks on the right merge with the road at a stone called the Headless Cross. This is an example of a medieval waymark, now sadly mutilated by time and erosion. Follow the road, turning left at the next junction, and finally arriving at the place where the track over the moorland emerged.

From here the road descends to the village via precipitous rocky bends, amid all the traditional flowers of the countryside—a typical Devon lane, untouched as yet by our old enemy, progress.

Once more we pass the entrance to Halscombe Farm, and find ourselves safely home. There are some good pubs in Moretonhampstead, namely the White Horse, The White Hart, and The Bell, and various tea shops; enjoyable research has been made at both Mearsdon Manor and The Gateway Tea Rooms.

WALK 8

LUSTLEIGH.

A 6 mile loop walk, with an alternative 3½ mile loop.

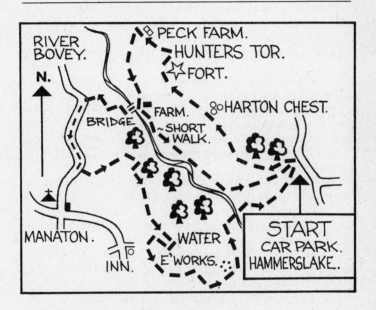

How to get there: No. 16 bus from Bovey Tracey.

Refreshments: At Becky Falls.

The village of Lustleigh, half a mile off the Bovey Tracey to Moretonhampstead road, A382, is a most attractive walking area, combining fields, country lanes and open moorland. It can be reached by a No. 16 bus from Bovey Tracey.

The starting point of these two loop walks is Hammerslake, to the northwest of Lustleigh, and arrived at via Lower Combe. Cars may be parked in a small layby in this quiet country road, where a footpath is signed into surrounding woodland. Take the path marked Hunter's Tor up through the trees and bear right, emerging on the top of a ridge with impressive moorland views. Follow this clear path along the top, heading northwest, and passing the outcrop of rock called Harton Chest, finally arriving at the ancient camp on Hunter's Tor. The circle is plainly outlined. Here the way is through a gate waymarked with the familiar orange dot. Bear right descending the hillside towards Peck Farm below, where a signposted gate (Lustleigh Cleave) takes us through the yard and down a track to another footpath sign. Left here, avoiding the cart track, right, inside the gate, and head for Foxworthy Bridge. This is an attractive farm lane, with easy walking, and brings us to beautiful Foxworthy Mill and farm. Here the loops split up, the shorter one passing through the yard and heading south east.

This way lies along the valley floor of Lustleigh Cleave slowly climbing due east around the shoulder of Sharpitor, then joining another path from lower down the Cleave, and emerging at the junction of paths at Hammerslake where the walk began.

The longer loop leaves Foxworthy behind and crosses the Bridge just beyond the farm, following up the private farm road and then turning left into the county road which leads to Manaton. Here, the village green affords rest after the steep hill.

The return loop of this longer walk takes us back the way we have come—after suitable resting time—and turns right opposite the Village Hall, into Slinkers Lane. This lane may be wet in bad weather, but provides good walking and is an excellent example of one of the old trackways with which Devon is blessed.

At the T junction turn right to the old-world buildings of Water. Here, if required, a detour may be made to the Kes Tor Inn not far down the Bovey Tracey road, where the bar snacks are good. If no detour is made, then we continue past the little "green" of Water and then turn left into the old Manaton Road, walking southeast, passing Beckhams Farm and finally descending a tunnel-like rough track at the bottom of which a gate proclaims private woodland. This path soon links up with the orange dots at a footpath four-way sign.

Another detour may be made here, if tea is required. A clear path is signed right to Becky Falls, where a popular cafe is sited just above the tumbling waters.

The loop walk, however, turns left at the four-way sign and ascends a clear way through woodland, passing an old earthworks on the verge of Hound Tor Wood, finally running down to Clam Bridge, an old packhorse way, through woods that form part of a nature reserve.

Over the Bridge the track bears right, but we go on up the hill, halfway up turning right into woodland and eventually finding a footpath signed to Hammerslake, our point of departure for both walks.

Lustleigh, below Hammerslake, offers The Cleave Hotel and Primrose Cottage tea rooms to the walker seeking refreshment.

WALK 9

MANATON TO EASDON DOWN.
A 4 mile walk.

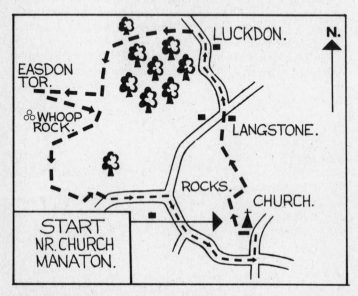

How to get there: By bus from Bovey Tracey.

Refreshments: At Becky Falls.

Manaton is a typical, rather remote, fringe-of-the-Moor village approximately 5 miles south of Moretonhampstead, and the same distance north of Bovey Tracey. It has a nice 15th century Church and warmly thatched old houses ringing the capacious green; as a starting point for many walks it is ideal, catering for the intrepid moor-walker as well as those who prefer the easy leisure of lanes and footpaths. It can be reached by the B3344 road from Bovey Tracey, and the B3212 from Moretonhampstead, which joins the B3344 at Beetor Cross.

This walk is a short, easy ramble of some 4 miles, which

encompasses moorland, country lane and footpath. Cars may be parked on convenient verges within the village. The Kes Tor Inn, half a mile down the road towards Bovey Tracey, is a pleasant place with bar snacks and a car park. Further down the road still and picturesquely placed in the trees, is the Becky Falls Cafe, again with its own car park.

Starting from the footpath sign outside Manaton Church, we cross the churchyard. Just inside the next gate stands a mutilated old medieval cross, a signpost from the past. The footpath turns right beyond the gate and leads us to nearby Manaton Rocks, where, in the spring, the bluebells are prolific and beautiful. From the top of the Rocks the view is almost panoramic on a clear day, with our next port of call, Easdon Tor, rising to the northwest. Following the arc south we see Hameldown in the far distance to the east, with the strange rock formation known as Bowerman's Nose rising up from Hayne Down in the near foreground. Who was Bowerman? Some say he actually lived, in William the Conqueror's day; others that the name is a derivation of the Celtic words for "great stone". Take your pick.

From Manaton Rocks we follow the path bearing right and join with another path leading northwest through pleasant country scenery, to Langstone Farm on the country road. Continue along the lane opposite Langstone to Lower Luckdon. Just beyond there is a gate and a signed footpath on the left—sometimes half hidden by overgrown foliage. Follow the orange dots to Easdon Hill. This path climbs steeply through a plantation and is hard going, arriving at a gate beyond which lies rough moorland.

Make a small diversion here by leaving the track and ascending to Easdon Tor (1,438ft.) and look at the countryside around and below. Just beneath the Tor a rock formation called Whooping Rock was supposed in the past to have miraculous powers of curing children suffering from whooping cough. There are Bronze Age hut circles and cairns as well as various boundary stones spread out on this slope of Easdon Down, which can provide interesting archeological discovery.

Leaving the Tor and returning to the path, we follow along beside a wall, turning left shortly and descending to the country road by way of a farm track entered left via a gate where a

Public Bridleway signs the way we have come from Lower Luckdon Farm. The track merges with the road below.

At Langstone Cross road junction take the Manaton road, returning to the village through pleasant farming scenery. A short walk, but quiet and full of beauty.

WALK 10

HAY TOR TO HOUND TOR
A loop walk of 7 miles, or alternative loop of 4 miles.

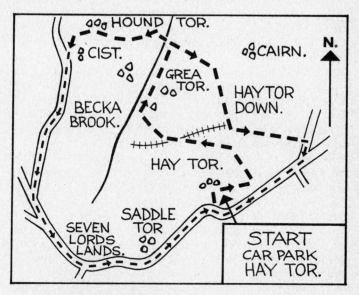

How to get there: By car.

Refreshments: Take a picnic or at Hay Tor Rocks.

This walk begins at the road below famous Hay Tor on the fringe of eastern Dartmoor and describes a circle of some 7 miles; rough going for the first half with ups and downs and some marshy ground, but keeping to the road for the remainder. The alternative loop is shorter and easier and keeps entirely to moorland.

The usual warning must be given about walking on Dartmoor, even though neither of these loop walks can place the walker in any danger; beware of mist, dress in weatherproof clothing, and take a map and compass.

31

From the rough car park below Hay Tor, climb to the rocks and then walk due east, joining a clear track northwest to Haytor Quarries. This track continues through the Quarry, leading to further workings beside Holwell Tor. Here granite was quarried and taken by horse-drawn trucks down the railway track laid in 1820, the remains of which can be seen when returning on the alternative, shorter loop of this walk.

From the Quarries we look northwest to the fearsome snarl of Greator Rocks, with Houndtor stark and jagged in the background. Immediately to our right Great Tor has a big outcrop of rock, with a logan stone hidden somewhere among its clutter. This is worth searching for, but takes time as it cannot be immediately pinpointed.

At the bottom of the valley the Becka Brook runs along between narrow banks and mossy boulders, widening out into a deep pool where the dam restricts it, and thereafter splashing down once more into its natural winding course.

We go down the slope and join the path that runs alongside the water until a footbridge carries the path over and upwards and here the alternative walk loops back, upwards, over one of the tracks that climb the hill of Haytor Down until, on the summit, Hay Tor rocks nearby may be used as a pivot on which to swing due south and join the disused granite railway track running down the slope almost due eastward. From here the car park will be visible and may be reached either by road or by moorland path.

The longer walk, however, crosses the footbridge mentioned above and climbs up, passing Greator Rocks, now on our left; the view from here takes in an angle of Hay Tor not usually seen, with Black Hill, Haytor Down behind us, and Trendlebere Down in the distance.

In the past this small valley with well-worn paths leading to Hound Tor must have been very active. On the hillside are the remains of a medieval settlement, some eleven dwellings in all, fairly recently excavated, and revealing beneath them earlier foundations. Hound Tor itself is perhaps the most spectacular pile of rock that one could hope to see; it looks primeval and unwelcoming, and many old tales quote it as being the haunt of that well-known inhabitant of the moor, the devil.

From the top of Hound Tor yet another view reveals itself,

this time Hameldown is lying like a stranded whale to the west, with the chunky piles of Honeybag Tor in the foreground. Aim at re-joining the road southwest of the rocks, and search for a ruined kistvaen, or burial place, in the heather. And this is not the only burial place in this immediate vicinity; three-quarters of a mile along this road to the east lies the grave of poor Kitty Jay, hanged in a nearby barn and for ever after banished to a lonely plot of ground in the middle of a moorland track. One of the typical Dartmoor stories says it is the pixies who keep her grave decorated with fresh flowers. Pixie or human, the flowers are always there.

The road now winds along in a half circle back to our starting place. It is possible to cut corners here and there, but the ground is often very wet. Look out, en route, for the fairy-castle-like profile of Bonehill Rocks, and for the square outlines of ancient cultivations at Foales Arrishes, under the hillside of Pil Tor where the roads meet at Hemsworthy Gate.

Seven Lords Land, where seven boundaries meet, lies to the left as the road sweeps onwards to Hay Tor. On the right Rippon Tor flies red flags when firing is in operation. Between Saddle Tor and Hay Tor there are boundary stones—and watch for the many varied faces that the rocks present . . . a sphinx, an Indian, the choice is yours.

The last view of this walk is different from what we have become used to, but equally magnificent; against the horizon the Haldon Belvedere stands out well and the coastline spreads itself to well beyond Berry Head, the Channel clear even on a grey day.

In the car park beneath Hay Tor Rocks there is usually an ice cream van which may even dispense tea and coffee. And the cafe just down the road provides splendid cream teas.

WALK 11

WIDECOMBE-IN-THE-MOOR.

Loop walk of 3 miles with alternative loop of 1½ miles.

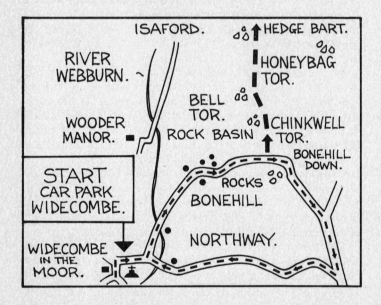

How to get there: By car.

Refreshments: At Widecombe.

Widecombe-in-the-Moor can be reached by car via the A384 road from Two Bridges to Ashburton, or the B3212 from Two Bridges to Moretonhampstead. A bus goes from Newton Abbot to Widecombe twice a week, on Wednesdays and Saturdays.

Most visitors to Dartmoor know and love Widecombe, with its handsome church, surrounding village green and attendant cluster of cafes and gift shops. But even Uncle Tom Cobley palls at times, and the walk up Bonehill and on to Honeybag

Tor does much to clear the mind of gimmicky grey mares and pixies, enabling the walker to see Widecombe in its proper perspective—as a jewel of a moorland village set amid the richness and ever-changing colours of the surrounding countryside.

This walk covers approximately 3 miles—but remember to add extra for all the hills you ascend. The way is mostly by road, although the alternative loop to Honeybag Tor and back is strictly moorland path. Be warned—these hills are breathtaking.

Passing out of Widecombe with the church on our right, we turn left on leaving the village. This is Bonehill, winding up out of the valley, bridging the East Webburn River, and fascinating visitors with its embellishment of enormous grey boulders and ancient farmsteads. There seems to be no record of why it is called Bonehill—nor of the derivation of the name Honeybag; these are mysteries that Dartmoor delights in, leaving much scope for the imagination of the walker.

The farms dotted on each side of Bonehill were all in existence by the 16th century, and at least one of them is a typical example of the original old "longhouse", when sheep-pen and dwellings were under the one roof. Even today, on Bonehill, the atmosphere of age is untouched.

At the top of the hill Bonehill Rocks loom large and spectacular on our right. The detour to Honeybag Tor takes us left here, up the track leading to the first tor with its rock basins, originally thought to be of Druid origin, but now known to be the result of erosion; so much for legend. This is Bell Tor, and for here the track continues to Chinkwell Tor, crowned with dilapidated cairns.

Cairns are generally connected with ancient burial grounds, and so we automatically look for hut circles which, sure enough, are scattered on the western side of the slope below the Tor. Above the circles is Slades Well, marked by a boundary stone. Here a spring forms a muddy pool where sheep and ponies drink.

North again towards Honeybag Tor, from the top of which an almost panoramic view opens up. On the west is the valley of Widecombe, with the village a mere cluster of houses crowding around the church. Behind us is Hound Tor with its ferocious facade of teeth-like rock. Northwards the ground slopes down to Hedge Barton, and on our left is the huge, whale-shaped ridge of Hameldown, marked by occasional bumps of barrows or burial grounds where Bronze Age chieftains were once laid to rest. Moormen used to say that from the top of Hameldown the whole of Devon could be seen. It's worth climbing to find out if the saying is true.

Return from Honeybag to Bonehill Rocks and then continue along the road leading southwest over Bonehill Down, turning sharp left at the next junction and returning to Widecombe by the more usual approach. Pleasant excursions may be made if wished on to the moorland to the left of this steep hill. Top Tor and Hollow Tor are easily reached and afford good resting places with excellent viewpoints.

Widecombe, at the bottom of the hill, has at least two tea houses, and also two pubs, the Old Inn, where bar snacks may be had, and the Rugglestone Inn which is just outside the village on the Venton road, a lovely little inn still keeping to its old way of life.

WALK 12

NEW BRIDGE.

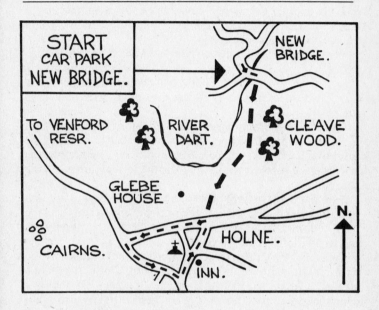

How to get there: By car.

Refreshments: At New Bridge.

New Bridge, one of the "honey-pot" areas of Dartmoor, spans the River Dart as it loops and wanders through the woods bordering the fringe of the moor. It stands on the Ashburton to Dartmeet road, (reached by the A38(T) from Exeter to Plymouth), a handsome grey stone bridge with three arches and pointed buttresses.

Beside it a large free car park usually has an ice cream van, with perhaps tea or coffee for a bonus. Two pleasant, shortish walks start from here, going in opposite directions, using footpaths and quiet lanes.

The first walk is a loop of 4 miles which begins by going through the iron gate at the north side of the bridge and following the bank of the river, with the lovely woodlands of Holen Chase to the right, and the rugged face of Leigh Tor to the left. Dominating the skyline is the eminence of Buckland Beacon, over 1,200ft.; on the stones at the summit of this tor are inscribed the Ten Commandments, and the view from that point is quite unforgettable.

When the path along the river joins the Buckland-in-the-Moor road, turn right for a short distance, passing Spitchwick Lower Lodge, then left at the fork guide-posted Lower Town, and look for a footpath to Poundsgate on the left as you climb the hill.

On reaching Poundsgate turn left along the road, and perhaps visit the Tavistock Inn, where once the devil, in the form of a horseman, stirred his beer with a fire and brimstone hoof, before he went on to Widecombe to reap havoc on the church there.

The road winds steeply down towards New Bridge through open moorland, and as you reach Leigh Tor you can leave the road and do a bit of scrambling before the bridge anticipates the second loop of this walk.

Crossing New Bridge there is a footpath to the woods on the right, proclaiming National Trust property. The path through glorious Cleave Woods winds on up, emerging in a meadow which takes the path on to the road above. Follow this road, running west towards Hexworthy. Notice "Glebe House", tucked away down a private drive, which is the house that marks the place where Charles Kingsley was born. The original Georgian vicarage was rebuilt in 1832. Although Kingsley only lived on Dartmoor for a short time, some of his writing surely reflects the magnificence and beauty of these moorland rivers, woods and tors.

Where this road joins the lower road from Holne, walkers with energy to spare may like to include a detour of another 4 miles, continuing northwest along the moorland road until lovely Venford Reservoir is reached, (2 miles and return walk of 2). Above the Reservoir, Bench Tor can easily be climbed; it hangs high and magnificent over the valley of the Dart—a reward indeed for the extra 4 miles involved in this detour.

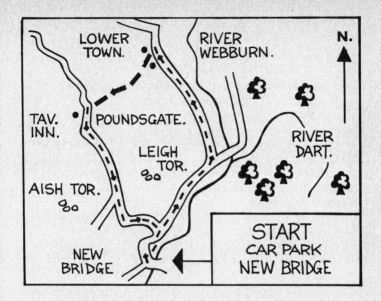

The original loop however turns left where the Hexworthy road joins the road to Holne, and we return to the village, where, turning left we find the old Church House Inn beside the little grey church. In the churchyard—notice the old stone stile—is an engaging tombstone, with an epitaph that has made Poor Old Ned quite famous.

The friendly village store, beside the church, keeps general provisions and sometimes even home-made cakes. The road goes north through the village, and then we turn right to find the entrance to the field through which the path goes back to New Bridge, via Cleave Woods.

WALK 13

DARTMEET

**A loop walk of 3 miles, with an additional loop
of another 3 miles.**

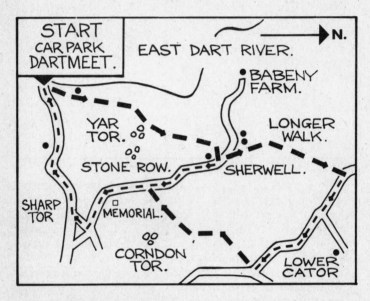

How to get there: By car.

Refreshments: At Badgers Holt.

Perhaps the most famous beauty spot on Dartmoor, Dartmeet—at the confluence of the waters of the East and West Dart Rivers—lies on the A384 road from Ashburton to Two Bridges. It has a large free carpark, with facilities for buying tea and soft drinks during the summer. Badger's Holt cafe, at the further end of the carpark, provides excellent cream teas; again, this is only open seasonally.

Dartmeet, with its historic clapper bridge and tumbling waters lapping the grey boulders, is very beautiful; but the holiday-makers sitting in parked cars seem to forget that even more beauty awaits them just out of sight. On this walk the way lies parallel with the river beyond Badger's Holt to begin with, but soon the path ascends north east, hugging the side of Yar Tor, and finally arriving at the road to Sherwell and Babeny from Ollsbrim, by way of the Sherwell enclosures.

Too much adventurous foraging away from this signed footpath will result in ploughing through boggy land down by the river, through shoulder-high bracken, which, although exhilarating, can also be very frustrating and time-absorbing.

The path reaches the road by way of a gate, and nearly opposite this the footpath continues on its way to Cator Gate, across the moor; this is the additional loop of 3 miles. The path is signed "Footpath to Country Road at Cator Gate, 1 mile", and is an easy track to follow, joining the country road at the entrance to the old tenement of Riddon. Turn right here and continue along the road. Opposite a road leading down to Shallowford, a cement milk platform marks the beginning of the return path over Corndon. The way is straight and steep, a clear track heading for a thorn tree. Continue, inclining slightly to the left, and passing between 2 cairns. The views from this point are magnificent. Follow the downward track towards the road, joining it only a small distance away from the start of this loop, i.e. near to the Sherwell enclosures, at which point the two loops unite and return to Dartmeet as one.

The first loop turned right when it emerged onto the road, and led through the lovely old buildings of Sherwell farm. The road winds along between Corndon Tor and Yar Tor; the views are very fine and one can play the familiar game of naming the many landmarks. In particular, Sharp Tor, with its unmistakeable shape, is eye-catching.

Beneath the cairns on top of Corndon Tor, and a little further along the road, just past the point where our additional loop has rejoined us, paths run up the hillside to the memorial raised to Lt. E. A. Cave-Penny, who died in Palestine in 1918, aged 19. Opposite this cross, on the slopes of Yar Tor, lies another burial place, between 2 and 3 thousand years old; a Bronze Age cist called the Moneypit. Not far from the road, the cist, set within a retaining circle of stones, lies near the remnants of a triple stone row. Many of these stones were vandalized by road and wallbuilders in the last century, and the rows are not easy to trace now. They lead north-westward to a barrow, and provide a fascinating exercise in detection.

The lower slopes of Yar Tor hold evidence of other primitive habitation; there is one particularly large hut circle, and another on the opposite side of the main road running down to Dartmeet, close by the track leading to Rowbrook Farm.

Other, more modern farmers, also worked this ground, and it is said that potatoes were grown here during the Napoleonic wars. There may be furrows and lynchets beneath the bracken, but these, like the old stones, take some finding.

The hill now winds steeply down to Dartmeet, with many more hut circles and enclosure remains dotted about it; the famous coffin stone hides itself on the opposite side of the road—a memory of days gone by when funeral processions rested their heavy loads on the long, low slab of rock, and small crosses and initials were cut into the stone by the bearers as they rested.

Back at Dartmeet be sure to inspect the old clapper bridge and listen to the river singing. The old saying has a certain chill about it . . . "River of Dart, River of Dart, Every year thou claimest a heart."

WALK 14

TWO BRIDGES

A loop walk of 3¼ miles, or alternative loop of 4½ miles.

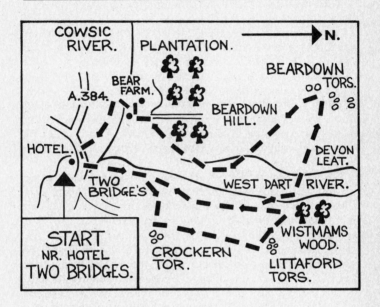

How to get there: By car.

Refreshments: At the Bridge Cafe.

Two Bridges is not even a village; situated at the junction of two roads traversing Dartmoor—the A384 and the B3212—it consists of (naturally) two bridges, an hotel and a few cottages.

The walk begins at the point between the cottage and the quarry opposite the hotel, heading through the gate, up the track to Crockern Cottage, then bearing right towards Crockern Tor, duly noticing the warnings of Ministry of Defence artillery and rifle practice. Watch for red lights and flags during times other than August or summer weekends.

Crockern Tor, with its slablike rocks, needs only a touch of imagination to picture the Stannary Parliament of the old tinning industry that was once held here, the rocks themselves providing tables and chairs. The view from here is beautiful, south-eastern Dartmoor spreading itself around, with the road below ribboning along to distant Princetown.

Turn back now and head along the ridge towards Littaford Tors. Just below the wall this side of these Tors are the remains of a prehistoric enclosure and hut circles. Other hut circles are scattered on each side of the West Dart River, which winds along at the bottom of these slopes.

Wistman's Wood is a Nature Conservancy Forest Nature Reserve, one of three areas of oakwood growing at a high altitude on Dartmoor. A cluster of enormous stones protect the dwarfed trees and produce a rich growth of mosses and lichens. The word Wistman, it seems, has alternative derivations—it can either mean stony wood by water, or wood of the Celts. Take your pick.

Here the shorter loop walk now returns to Two Bridges, picking a way along the sometimes wet ground beside the river. If the track becomes boggy, the walker is advised to climb to the left, where a path can be found on dry turf.

The longer walk crosses the river by any of the natural stepping stones—taking great care if the water should be running very high. On the other side, the rough, steep side of Bear Down is quite a challenge. Up we go, again avoiding the circles of bog, easy to see by the vivid greenery of moss and rush. The flora here is interesting, with stunted gorse bushes and small patches of heather and whortleberry bushes. Overhead buzzards soar and perhaps a heron flaps heavily down the stream. It doesn't require much imagination to think of Bronze Age ladies rinsing out their smalls in the river below.

Half way up this slope the Devonport Leat loops around the contours, a footpath keeping it company. This was built in 1794 to take drinking water to Devonport Dockyard. There are occasional projecting stones in the leat walls which are sheep jumps, whereby walkers may cross over on their ascent up to Bear Down Tors, where wonderful views of the Moor stretching as far as the eye can see are a reward for aching legs after the steep climb.

The way back to Two Bridges is downhill and easy. Follow the ridge southwards to a wall which eventually reaches a gate. Here the path passes into the silent gloom of Bear Down Plantation via a footbridge across the Leat. Once out of the Plantation the orange dots and notice boards of Dartmoor National Park take over and the track is clearly defined through Bear Down Farm.

Pause at Cowsic Bridge to look back and see a restored clapper bridge upstream. Follow the river through a very beautiful valley of enormous beech trees; here the Cowsic River splashes and leaps among vast boulders. Stone steps lead the way over a wall and thence across a field, and there you are, home and dry, at Two Bridges after a strenuous 4½ miles.

Two Bridges Hotel will provide refreshment.

WALK 15

FERNWORTHY FOREST, near CHAGFORD.
2 loop walks of 5¼ miles and 6½ miles.

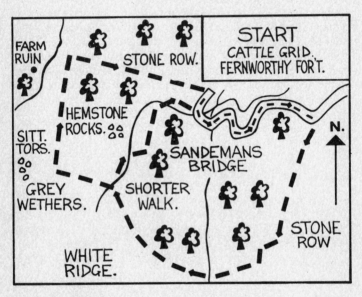

How to get there: By bus from Newton Abbot.

Refreshments: At Chagford.

Fernworthy Forest, clustered beside a reservoir, is some 3 miles from Chagford, one of Dartmoor's ancient Stannary towns. Chagford may be reached by No. 16 bus from Newton Abbot, or No. 19 bus from Exeter, and by car via the A382 road from Moretonhampstead to Whiddon Down. There are hotels, inns and tea houses at Chagford, but not at Fernworthy.

These two walks describe various-sized semi-circles around the perimeter of the Forest, with spectacular views from every angle. They strike out, from forest track, to the open Moor to explore Bronze Age antiquities, and climb a tor of 1,764 ft. to

46

achieve a truly panoramic view. The way includes steep ascents, marshy, rough ground, and ends by returning via an easy track down the centre of the Forest.

The walk starts just inside the cattle grid at the entrance of the Forest, where cars may be parked on the verge. Fernworthy Reservoir lies to the north and northwest of this point. The way lies **outside** the Forest, hugging the edge and following the conifers around, leaving the Reservoir behind, a small lake quite lovely in its unnatural surroundings. Before the trees were planted, this was a bare sweep of Moor; in the 17th century the three farmsteads existing here were referred to as a village. And back in the Bronze Age it was the home of the first Dartmoor settlers. The remains of their civilisation—cairns, hut circles, stone rows and burial places—still litter the Moor, some of them lying within the Forest bounds.

Varied views delight on this trek beside the trees as the walk takes us first due south, then southwest and, turning the corner, suddenly northwest and into the teeth of the wind if it happens to be that sort of weather. The ground is boggy in places, particularly where small streams flow into the Forest.

Having ascended, and then left, Assycombe Hill, negotiated the wet tussocks at the tip of the Forest and then laboriously climbed up White Ridge, we then descend to a ford close by an entrance to the Forest. Hut circles and pounds can be explored in the immediate vicinity and are marked on the Ordnance Survey Map.

Here an obvious path strikes out due west and upwards, taking us to the ridge in the middle of which stand the two stone circles known as the Grey Wethers. These were undoubtedly erected as part of religious rites by the early settlers, but little is known of their exact purpose. Another track crosses the circles heading due south and Postbridge, not far away.

Above the Grey Wethers is Sittaford Tor—a climb that is steep and rough because of the tussocky ground; but the view from the summit is magnificent, with all the familiar peaks of Dartmoor laid out around us.

Old Teignhead farm, sheltered by its clump of trees, lies to the north, just below the Tor, with the infant North Teign River flashing and shining as it meanders through the valley below the farm. Built at the end of the 18th century, Teignhead was

47

once a thriving farmstead with solid outhouses, the warm, low ceilinged kitchen the hub of family life. Farm carts rolled noisily over the stone bridge across the river. Now the place is derelict, the stones lying untidily around the bare bones of the old house, the only signs of life the clusters of sheep and ponies cropping the turf that increasingly encroaches on what was once a home. It's worth making a detour to explore this old ruin.

Beyond the farm, the northern moors curve away into the distance, with their desolate peat bogs and attendant firing range notices. Famous Cranmere Pool, the so-called heart of the Moor, lies within these bogs. It is dangerous and illegal to enter land within the firing range when red flags—at night, red lights—are showing. Times of firing can be ascertained from local Post Offices and Police Stations.

The shorter ending to this walk is to return from the Grey Wethers to the Forest and take the track close to the ford which leads northeast to Sandeman's Bridge, (inside the Forest), and then follow the road which returns to the parked car at the Forest entrance; this loop is approximately 5¼ miles in all.

Alternatively, the slightly longer way back takes us down from Sittaford Tor and through a gate in the wall, along a path leading up to another Forest entrance opposite Teignhead farm. Here the track is downhill and easy; various firebreaks and other Forestry paths enable the walker to explore among the trees for Bronze Age antiquities at Hemstone Rocks, (west), and at Assycombe Hill, (south). The track ends at a gate close to the Reservoir edge, from where a road returns us to the parked car and the point of commencement. This loop is approximately 6½ miles. The way back through Fernworthy Forest can be a strange experience. From the vastness of the Moor we step into the quiet shadowed path between the trees, with the light making weird patterns down the maze of tunnels and firebreaks.

Leaving the Forest is like shutting the door of a lonely house; visit Fernworthy and see for youself what magic Dartmoor can evoke.

WALK 16

THE TEIGN GORGE

A loop walk of 4½ miles, with a possible added detour of 2 miles.

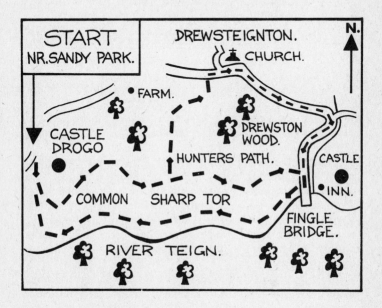

How to get there: By car.

Refreshments: At Drewston Common.

The river Teign runs between steep, tree-clad slopes of the Teign Gorge just a mile due south of the picturesque village of Drewsteignton, providing excellent walking, both on the heights of the slopes and along the riverside. This is romantic, evocative countryside, and the footpaths afford a wealth of possible loop-walks and leisurely explorations.

Cars may be parked on the stony verge of the road that winds up from Sandy Park (where there is a splendid Inn), 2 miles northeast of Chagford, to Drewsteignton. Just short of the entrance to Castle Drogo a gate demands that you PLEASE shut it. Follow the farm path towards Coombe Farm and Gibhouse and then, by some shady beech trees, go through another gate heading left and upwards, along the bridleway signed as "Hunter's Path" to Fingle Bridge.

Castle Drogo, recently acquired by the National Trust, now open to the public every day from April to the end of October hides itself behind a sparse fringe of pine trees above us. The path emerges, via bracken and heather, on to the summit of Hunter's Tor, where there is an excellent view of the surrounding lush countryside, with Dartmoor's humps and bumps beyond.

Follow this path around the horseshoe bends, with the ground falling gradually away on the right to the depths of the Gorge: far below the sun occasionally strikes a glint of water, and sometimes pin-people may be seen making their way along the lower Fisherman's Path—our own route back.

Along the Hunter's Path, an unsigned track runs sharply off to the left, climbing uphill among the bracken fronds. This leads to Drewsteignton, and is a possible loop detour of 2 miles. It crosses fields and woodland, heading north, eventually joining a distinct footpath between high hedges, and emerging at the entrance to the village. Here the walker should loiter awhile, enjoying the lovely old cottages, and the sombre beauty of the grey church.

A mile-long, downhill road, leads out of the village to Fingle Bridge, where it joins up with the end of the Hunter's Path, as it comes out onto the road just above the Bridge.

But if we ignore the detour to Drewsteignton, the Hunter's Path continues on its dizzy course, going to Fingle by way of a hunting gate above Sharp Tor, and thence to Drewston Common, arriving at its destination close to the car park of the Angler's Rest Free house and Restaurant, where excellent refreshments of all varieties are offered, guaranteed to tickle the palate of the most jaded walker.

On the site of the Angler's Rest there was originally an old mill. Here the accommodating miller built a "parlour" and a kitchen, where visiting travellers were allowed to prepare their own provisions. After the mill, a tea house occupied the site, run by two Victorian ladies. There are some interesting old pictures inside the Angler's Rest which show, not only the tea house, but the original mill. Fingle Bridge is alive with history.

Across the old Bridge, built in the 16th century to take packhorses on their weary way to market, there is an area of woodland where the public may enjoy itself. Here again, footpaths abound. The zig-zag route up to Cranbrook Castle may not be everybody's cup of tea on a hot day, but the view at the end of it, when the rough-clad ramparts are reached a thousand feet above the river, is reward enough for the demanding climb.

Our chosen way back—the Fisherman's Path—lies close to the chuckling River Teign, cavorting between grey boulders and superb tree-lined slopes which unfold one after the other, pale green leaves merging with darker ones into a canopy of arboreal lace. This is not an easy path, for all its beauty; stones and intrusive roots can wrench an ankle all to quickly.

Just beyond the little weir and subsequent footbridge, the path divides, the left fork going on to Chagford via Dogmarsh Bridge, and our way taking us up beside Gibhouse and then back to the starting place.

Drewsteignton has no tea rooms, but during licensing hours the Drew Arms is worthy of a visit—one of the few remaining village pubs.

WALK 17

BUCKFASTLEIGH

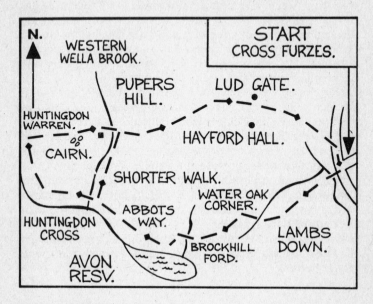

How to get there: By car.

Refreshments: In Buckfastleigh.

Famed for Buckfast Abbey, founded and endowed by Canute, Buckfastleigh is a village sprawled around the busy A38 (T) road, between Ashburton and South Brent. Its environs, on the south-east fringe of Dartmoor, provide wonderful walking. This is a loop walk of 5 miles, with an alternative extra 2 miles if required, over hilly moorland with breath-taking scenery.

Take the Wallaford Down road westward out of Buckfastleigh to Cross Furzes. Cars may be left on a useful verge. Follow the signposted path over the ford, and then bear southwest, looking for the orange-tipped posts which take us over Lambs Down, crossing a small tributary of the Dean Burn and eventually arriving at Water Oak Corner. Here, remembering to shut the gate as requested, bear almost due west, following the track to Brockhill Ford.

This is the ancient track known as the Abbots Way; a "post-road" travelled by the old Cistercian monks, who were all wool traders, when taking their wares to Plymouth, and a useful path linking Buckfast Abbey with Buckland Abbey, (southwest Dartmoor).

Leaving Brockhill Ford, as it feeds into the Avon Reservoir, follow the Abbots Way through a large enclosed hut group, passing also a kistvaen. The track winds down the hill, following the Avon River upstream, with Bishops Mead on the opposite side bare and sparse. At the confluence of the Wallabrook with the Avon there stands Huntingdon Cross, and here the Abbots Way crosses the river by clapper bridge and slopes away uphill, in the direction of Princetown.

Our way now divides, the shorter loop bearing north-eastwards following along beside the Western Wella Brook, and exploring the many mining relics that litter the moorland. Watch for pit holes and overgrown gulleys of the old workings. The pits are deep and open and dangerous, but there is much to be seen, exploring among the leats and channels and deserted buildings.

West of us, Huntingdon Warren with its cairn, the Heap of Sinners, is a reminder of the past, when rabbits were brought over from Europe by the Normans. Although meant for sport, they also provided welcome food for the tinminers living in remote parts of the moor. Most warrens were controlled by a warrener living nearby, and Warren House, a ruin on the hillside, was such a dwelling.

This loop bears east and then northeast, joining a clear path down towards Lud Gate, one of the oldest moorland gates, and then a mile long track winds back to Furzes Cross.

The longer loop, which takes in an extra 2 miles of moorland, proceeds upstream from Huntingdon Cross, exploring the humpy mounds and gulleys of the mine workings, long since deserted. In the past this was a busy area, with tin miners living hard rough lives in constant friction with the elements. Opposite spectacular Broad Falls there is the remains of a blowing house, and it is not difficult to imagine how water was diverted, by leat, to power the machinery necessary to convert the ore into ingots, ready to be transported by pony back to the market towns. Now only the scars among the heather and turf, with the piles of littered stones, remain as an indication of a past industry.

The River continues up to Avon Head, rising somewhere in the folds of the far hills, but we turn east, following a deep gulley and climbing steadily through rough moorland until we reach the summit of Huntingdon Warren, the cairn called the Heap of Sinners. Pause here for breath and to add the traditional stone to the cairn.

The way back is downhill, descending due east from the cairn and passing through the ruins of Warren House, eventually joining up with the shorter loop as it returns via Lud Gate to Furzes Cross.

Buckfastleigh has some friendly pubs and at least one tea room.

WALK 18

POWDERHAM and KENTON.

A 3¼ loop walk, with an addition of a 2 mile river walk.

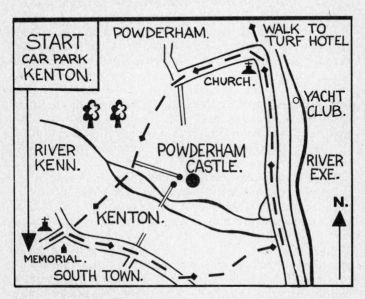

How to get there: By bus from Exeter or Newton Abbot.

Refreshments: In Powderham Inns.

Kenton, the home of Powderham Castle, is a small village on the busy A379 coast road from Exeter to Newton Abbot. The number 2 bus will take you there. Cars may be parked at the side of a small triangle of land enclosing the War Memorial in the centre of the village, where this loop walk begins. There are no cafes in the village, but the general store sells soft drinks in bottles, and a variety of groceries. The Devon Arms and the Dolphin inns offer refreshment in licencing hours.

This walk, though beginning along the busy main road—do watch how you cross—soon turns off through footpaths into a quiet country road, and also, if desired, extends the route for 2 extra miles along the River Exe.

Leaving the War Memorial turn right and follow the A379 for nearly half a mile, passing the entrance to Powderham Castle. This small but captivating stately home is open to the public daily, except on Fridays and Saturdays, from 26th May to 12th September every year, and in the summer months holds displays of falconry, jousting, etc. on one Sunday each month.

Having passed the entrance to the Castle, a footpath will be seen starting at a kissing-gate opposite Old Jail House in the part of the village called Southtown. This path crosses a meadow diagonally, from west to east, emerging on to a farm path by a footpath sign directing us across the field ahead, this time in a north-easterly direction. A small wooden stile takes the footpath through nettles to an iron gate opening onto the road beside the River Exe. At the time of writing no footpath sign has yet been erected at this point, although it may occur at any moment.

This pleasant road meanders along beside the river, with Powderham Castle and its magnificent deerpark on our left. Between the river and the road the railway runs past, with a view of the old pumping house at Starcross behind us, a memory of Brunel's Atmospheric Railway. In winter and wet weather this road is sometimes flooded, but on a fine day it provides easy walking with magnificent views all around. On the opposite side of the River Exe, Lympstone is a picturesque huddle between redstone cliffs, while Exmouth's grey, spreading sprawl reaches down to the sea at the river mouth.

At low tide the birdlife on the mudflats of the estuary is enormously varied; solitary herons may often be seen fishing the streams in the deerpark or roosting in the trees, and the Castle herd of fallow deer wander at will beneath the huge trees. The Castle itself can be glimpsed from this road—a small, squat building that contains its medieval origins within restored walls.

The road passes Starcross Yacht Club and, opposite it, a grown-over private entrance to the Castle grounds. Where the road turns sharply left, a footpath on the right signs the way to the river walk, a detour of 2 miles which unfortunately cannot be extended into a loop, as it abuts on private land.

This detour crosses the railway line—(keep your eyes open for trains)—and follows the river as the path leads us along its banks, and up to the Turf Hotel and the beginning of the Exeter Canal. Built in 1566, this Canal was made to resolve the problem of the weir thrown across the river by the Countess of Devon, who was displeased with the citizens of Exeter and thus stopped their trading facilities. With the advent of this, the first lock canal in the country, Exeter was once again made accessible to shipping and trade.

Bird watchers really come into their own on this added walk, and if timed for late afternoon it is very exciting to watch the birds coming down to the water. Duck, geese, curlew and oyster catcher fill the air with their voices, and the river becomes full of churning wings. Beyond the Turf Hotel footpaths lead on to Exeter, but although a track leads across the railway line in the direction of Powderham, this is a private road and does NOT grant access to walkers. We must, therefore, retrace our steps to the road that now turns right to Powderham Church, and the loop that will take us back to Kenton.

Powderham Church is made of red sandstone, and is, so we are told, listed as "one of the treasures of England." It is full of memories of long dead Courtenays, and crowned by a medieval weather-vane in the shape of a dolphin. The enormous oak trees that shade the church entrance have yielded up cannon balls, relics of the Civil War, when Cromwell's troops besieged and occupied both Castle and church.

Passing the church, the long, tree-lined avenue leads up towards another entrance to the Castle, and some beautiful pink cottages. A notice on a tree in this avenue says "snakes, be warned"—but whether this means what it says or is merely a ploy to keep intrusive walkers from the verges of the road is anyone's guess.

On the hill facing us stands an old belvedere, whose all-seeing eye rakes the river and the hills beyond. With the Castle entrance on our left, we take the signed footpath that runs up the side of the field beneath the belvedere, towards a ridge of woodland. Beside the trees the path descends again, with the deerpark on its left. Here, on a hot day, the deer often graze in the shade of the superb old trees. There are some immense sweet chestnuts, with twisted boles and limbs; the path is littered with wild flowers and rhododendron bushes. With peeps of the Castle to our left, we seem to be back in the more leisured, pastoral, past.

A gate takes the path across a track and down into water-meadows, where South Devon cows graze, and occasional thatched cottages enchant the eye. A bridge carries us across the River Kenn and eventually onto a path bordering a new housing estate. This path deposits us on the pavement of the A379 road, just opposite the War Memorial. Suddenly we have left the past, and are back to reality.

Before leaving Kenton, spare time to visit All Saints parish church, which has some remarkably beautiful furnishings, and dates from 1360, with evidence of an earlier church erected in 560.

On this walk, we have been treading some of the original byways of medieval England.

WALK 19

TEIGNMOUTH TO DAWLISH.

5 mile walk, with alternative loop of 4½ miles, or shorter loop of 3½ miles which includes return from Dawlish by bus.

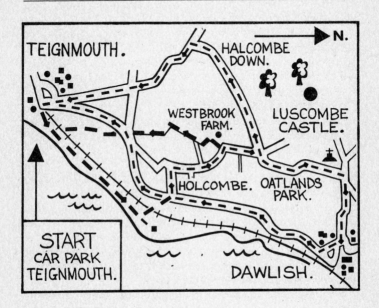

How to get there: Bus, train or car.

Refreshments: In Teignmouth or Dawlish.

The seawall at Teignmouth—reached by the A379 road from Exeter; by train, or by bus from Exeter or Torquay—is the starting point of this walk, which encompasses both flat and hilly walking on country roads and farm tracks, with an alternative bus ride back from Dawlish should the walker be so inclined.

Paid car parks are numerous in Teignmouth, as are hotels, pubs and tea houses. The wall leads us towards Dawlish, and runs alongside Brunel's famous railway—the line that revolutionized tourist traffic to the west country. It was completed in 1847 and called The Atmospheric Railway, making use of air pressure to propel trains at a maximum speed of 64 miles an hour. Pumping stations were built at regular intervals along the track—such a tower still stands on the other side of Dawlish, at Starcross Station.

The walk along the wall is extremely pleasant, with sheltering redstone cliffs above, swathed in greenery and wild flowers, and a variety of bird life to watch when the tide is right. At certain conditions of low tide there is the opportunity of searching the surface of the beach for traces of the salt pans which were the source of Teignmouth's first industrial venture far back in history.

The little triangle of rock and land known as Sprey Point halfway along the wall was formed by a cliff fall in the last century. On a clear day there is a good view, from the Ore Stone (off the furthermost point to the east), to Portland in the west, as we look out to sea.

The end of the wall falls short of a famous rock formation called the Parson and the Clerk, which, legend tells us, is all that was left of a Dawlish vicar and his clerk who dared to defy the Devil. Even more striking is Shag Rock, usually crowned with sea birds. Steps lead from the wall into Smuggler's Cove—but don't attempt this at high tide. The echoes of history sound all around us here, as we pass beneath the railway and ascend the steep and narrow Smuggler's Lane.

The main road to Exeter streams past here, a very dangerous crossing, and the opposite, quieter, road leads us into the old-world village of Holcombe. Turn right and climb up to the Castle Inn for timely refreshment if required. A peaceful country lane winds through well-wooded banks from here and passes Westbrook Farm. Here the walker must decide whether to return to Teignmouth by bus or on foot.

If a bus ride is decided on, climb the hill past the Farm and then turn right down Oak Hill to the parish church of St. Gregory in the neighbouring village of Dawlish. It is worth making a detour through the churchyard to attractive Newhay Falls behind, where the spirit of old rural Dawlish still lives on. To finish this loop of the walk, follow the river through

Dawlish's public gardens until the sea front is reached, when a no. 2 bus, (also no. 13 in summer only), can be caught back to Teignmouth.

Alternatively, the walk may be completed on foot by turning left at the junction of Oak Hill and Holcombe Down Road, and following this latter road along a tree-lined ridge which affords magnificent views on each side, and turning left at the T-junction at its end. Here we descend via a steep, rough, but metalled road into a pleasant housing estate, and so down to the junction of New Road and Woodway Road in Teignmouth. By following Woodway Road straight downhill we join the main Exeter Road and can reach the sea wall—our point of departure—by crossing the large car park on the left of this road some hundred yards above the church of St. Michael on the seafront.

The last alternative, which will complete the 5 mile version of this walk, is to turn in at the entrance to Westbrook Farm on the road out of Holcombe, and following the rough path (muddy in wet weather) that veers left and upwards. This eventually joins a larger track coming in from the left. Continue, keeping left at next fork. This is pleasant walking, along a grassy track, with sea views on the left. Go down the hill, passing farm outbuildings where the going is marshy after rain, and then uphill, finally emerging in the Teignmouth fringe of Holcombe village at Oakhill Cross Road, by Turnpike Cottage.

Cross the road here—again, this is a dangerous crossing—and follow Cliff Road, which is a quiet path running down to Teignmouth via the railway bridge, where the seawall begins.

One other pleasant diversion is to turn right, immediately after an ancient kissing-gate, into Rowdens Public Gardens, where beautiful trees retain an old-fashioned atmosphere. Here we can join the main Exeter Road at the Beacon School, and turn left towards Teignmouth's sea front, and the familiar seawall.

WALK 20

THE RIVER TEIGN ESTUARY

A loop walk of 4 miles plus an additional loop of 2½ miles.

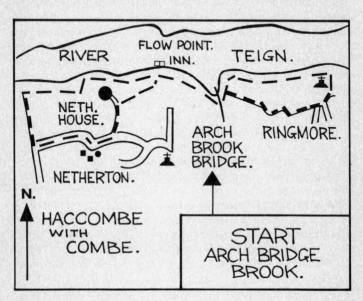

How to get there: By bus from Teignmouth.

Refreshments: At Ringmore.

The estuary of the River Teign has attractive, unfrequented country on its southern banks and provides interesting walking for those who like something a little out of the ordinary. Attention must be paid to tide tables, and it is advisable to wait until at least one hour after high tide before starting this walk along the river beach. Even in summer there is plenty of mud and wet sand, and so shoes must be strong and waterproof. Do NOT walk when the tide is coming in.

A good point to start either of these two loop walks is at Arch Brook Bridge, 1½ miles due west of the small village of

Ringmore, an extension of Shaldon, which lies on the opposite bank of the river from Teignmouth on the mouth of the estuary. The number 116 bus travels from Teignmouth to Newton Abbot via Shaldon at approximately hourly intervals every day during the summer months, and can drop passengers at Arch Brook Bridge.

Here the river comes slightly inland to form a small creek, and cars may be parked safely on the road verge.

The first, and longer, loop follows the footpath that hugs the river bank going upstream towards Newton Abbot, beneath shady old trees growing out of redstone cliffs. Wading birds and seagulls haunt the muddy reaches of the Teign and the air is full of sound.

Follow this path until the inn at Coombe Cellars, (once a row of primitive fisherman's cottages, with a long history of smuggling,) is reached. Avoiding the outfall of surface water just beyond the inn, continue along the beach, enjoying the view up and down river. Almost opposite is the village of Bishopsteignton, with Haldon Moor above. Buckingham Palace is the name of a rock on the river bank below Bishopsteignton where, legend says, a crazy old man lived for many years.

At Netherton Point—recognisable by its flat spread of grass and ensuing inlet—it is advisable to cross the brook by climbing the low wall for a few yards. This part of the river is a haven for wildlife, and although the scar of a new road may be seen in the distance of the environs of Newton Abbot, the river itself seems to be remote and desolate.

Just over a mile from Coombe Cellars a definite track leads upwards from the river bank, and this is the beginning of the return leg of our loop walk. Follow this steep and often muddy path until it joins with a secondary road which turns sharp left and takes us, via winds and bends, through the ancient hamlet of Lower Netherton, full of eye-catching old farmhouses and cottages.

Having passed Lower Netherton, the road now forms a T-junction and we turn again left, along a minor road leading to Nethertown House. Just short of the entrance to this house there is a farm gate on the right-hand side which leads us into the footpath to Coombe Cellars. Follow the obvious track through the gate and into the next field, when the path hugs the hedge to the right, passing through another farm gate on our left, and then crossing the field obliquely to where the inn can be clearly seen in front of us. This path emerges onto the river bank, through a wooden fence-stile. The river path leads back to Arch Brook Bridge.

The second loop heads in the opposite direction to Ringmore, once again following the river path. Look out for a disused kiln hidden in the rocky cliffs that overshadow the beach; the story goes that there is a purse of gold hidden within, only to be found by one who visits the spot alone at midnight!

At Ringmore this walk may be completed by leaving the river and returning to Arch Brook Bridge via the winding road, perhaps stopping to visit the tucked-away church of St. Nicholas, which has a leper window close to the altar, and a magnificent sundial on the wall adjoining the porch.

This road passes between attractive old cottages—look out particularly for all that remains of the ancient farmstead of Teignharvey, and Little Harvey opposite.

These two walks are especially attractive on a hot summer day, when the cool serenity of the River Teign is a solace to both body and mind.